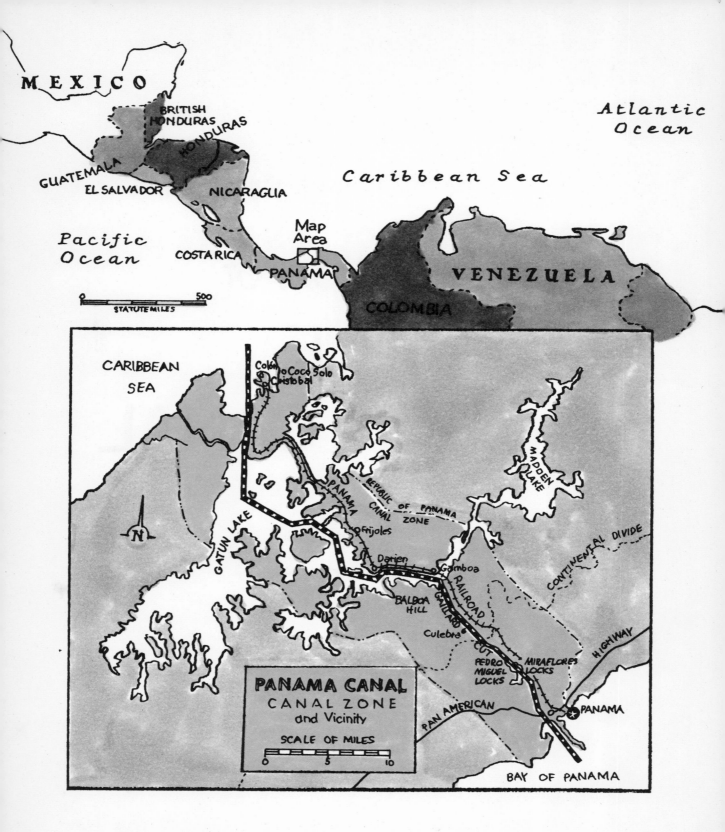

MEXICO

Atlantic Ocean

BRITISH HONDURAS

HONDURAS

GUATEMALA

EL SALVADOR

NICARAGUA

Caribbean Sea

Pacific Ocean

COSTA RICA

Map Area

PANAMA

VENEZUELA

COLOMBIA

500

STATUTE MILES

CARIBBEAN SEA

Colón Coco Solo
Cristóbal

GATUN LAKE

MADDEN LAKE

PANAMA CANAL

REPUBLIC OF PANAMA CANAL ZONE

Frijoles

CONTINENTAL DIVIDE

N

Darien

Gamboa

RAILROAD

BALBOA HILL

GAILLARD

Culebra

CUT

PEDRO MIGUEL LOCKS

MIRAFLORES LOCKS

HIGHWAY

PANAMA

PAN AMERICAN

PANAMA CANAL
CANAL ZONE
and Vicinity

SCALE OF MILES

0   5   10

BAY OF PANAMA

Cornerstones of Freedom

The Story of
THE
PANAMA CANAL

By R. Conrad Stein

Illustrated by Keith Neely

 CHILDRENS PRESS, CHICAGO

Library of Congress Cataloging in Publication Data

Stein, R. Conrad.
    The Story of the Panama Canal.

    (Cornerstones of freedom)
    Summary: A history of the building of one of
the world's great engineering feats.
    1. Panama Canal—History—Juvenile
literature. [1. Panama Canal—History]
I. Neely, Keith, R. ill. II. Title. III. Series.
F1569.C2S76   1982   972.87   82-4565
ISBN 0-516-04640-3   AACR2

On his fourth and last voyage to the New World, Christopher Columbus cruised along the coast of the present-day nation of Panama. He hoped to find a way to sail to China, India, and other lands of silks and spices. Columbus did not discover a passage. He returned to Spain in despair and died two years later. He never found out that Panama was a strip of jungle only about forty miles wide. Beyond that jungle spread an ocean that was the gateway to the East.

Spanish adventurers and gold seekers followed Columbus to the New World. One of them was Vasco Núñez de Balboa. In 1513 Balboa led a party across the jungles of Panama. He became the European discoverer of the Pacific Ocean.

Other Spaniards sailed the Pacific. They found Peru and the gold of the Inca. The gold-hungry Europeans raided Inca cities and took fabulous treasures. Using Indian slave labor, they built a mule trail across Panama. On that trail they transported gold from the Pacific to the Atlantic Ocean. For the next two hundred years the narrow mule path cutting through Panama was the crossroads of the mighty Spanish Empire.

A few Spaniards dreamed about digging a canal through Panama. A canal crossing the stem of land (called an isthmus) would create a shipping lane between the two oceans. But the Spaniards could not handle the enormous task of digging such a canal. Finally, their power in the New World diminished.

In the early 1800s the British, the French, and the new American nation all thought about building a Central American canal. While they thought, the jungle reclaimed the old Spanish mule path.

Then, in the mid 1800s, Panama suddenly became important again. Once more, the reason for its importance was gold. In 1848, a California ranch foreman stumbled on gold glittering in a streambed. People flocked to California. All were eager to become rich. One way for easterners to go there was to sail to Panama, cross the isthmus on foot and by raft, and then take a Pacific Ocean ship to California. The trip through the Panamanian jungle was dreadful. So a group of American businessmen

decided to build a railroad over the isthmus. They were sure they could make a lot of money. Construction began on the Panama Railroad in 1850. The railroad followed roughly the same course as the old Spanish mule trail.

The Americans soon discovered the painful lesson the Spaniards had learned in Panama. Building anything in Panama was practically impossible. Workers fainted in the noonday heat that reached 120 degrees Fahrenheit. Because it rained 250 days a year, the soil was usually mush. Worst of all,

Panama was a pesthole of insects. Swarms of mosquitoes buzzed everywhere. An American visitor named Selfridge once wrote that he observed "mosquitoes so thick I have seen them put out a lighted candle with their burnt bodies."

No one knew at that time that some of those mosquitoes were deadly. They carried malaria and yellow fever. Workers on the Panama Railroad became sick, lay in agony for days, and died. The exact number of railroad workers who died is unknown. But the Panama Railroad probably cost about six thousand lives. Miners in the California gold fields said that one worker died for every crosstie on the forty-seven-mile-long railroad.

The railroad through Panama was finally completed in 1855. Its owners made a fortune. In its first six years of operation, the one-track railroad earned seven million dollars.

Businessmen and governments around the world began thinking of the profits a Central American canal could earn. The governments of the United States and Great Britain argued. They almost went to war over the right to build an inter-ocean canal. But while Great Britain and America argued, France acted. In 1879 a group of French businessmen formed a company to dig a canal in Panama. At the time, Panama was a province of Colombia. The government of France made an agreement with Colombia allowing construction to begin. The great French adventure in Panama commenced.

Heading the French project was Ferdinand de Lesseps, a wealthy builder and engineer. Ten years earlier, he had built the marvelous Suez Canal in North Africa. Now de Lesseps turned his efforts from the sands of Egypt to the jungles of Panama. Also joining the company was a young Frenchman named Philippe Bunau-Varilla. He would later play a very important role in the United States canal project.

FERDINAND DE LESSEPS   FRENCH EXCAVATORS

With confidence and enthusiasm, the French began work in 1882. They hired an army of workers and shipped the most modern heavy equipment to Panama. Their efforts ended in a colossal flop.

After seven years of work, the French completed only two-fifths of a canal. Everything seemed to go wrong. Huge trenches dug through mountains would suddenly be filled in by mud slides. Overnight, the mud slides erased the work of months. And fatal diseases swept through the work force like wildfire.

The original French Panama Canal company went bankrupt in 1889. It sold its equipment to another French company. Philippe Bunau-Varilla was an officer in that company. The young Frenchman hoped to sell the company's holdings to the United States.

Certainly the United States wanted to build an inter-ocean canal. Americans had always resented the French efforts at building a canal in what they considered "their" part of the world. Americans also believed that a canal was essential for their defense. During the Spanish-American War in 1898, the United States battleship *Oregon* had to sail from San Francisco to Cuba. Because it had to make the thirteen-thousand-mile trip around South America, it arrived almost too late to take part in the war.

The Americans, however, wanted to build their canal through the country of Nicaragua. They thought they would have fewer construction problems there. Also, Nicaragua was farther north. A canal there would shorten the passage time between coasts.

The Americans changed their minds largely because of the efforts of Philippe Bunau-Varilla. Bunau-Varilla hoped to sell the Americans the millions of dollars of equipment the French had left in Panama. Also, Bunau-Varilla had an overwhelming belief in the wisdom of digging a Panama Canal.

Bunau-Varilla traveled to Washington and warned American Congressmen that Nicaragua's many volcanoes would destroy a canal constructed there. As proof that Nicaragua was volcano-ridden he gave every American senator a Nicaraguan postage stamp. On the stamp was a picture of a smoldering volcano. Then, just days before Congressional debate on the canal site, a volcano on the island of Martinique erupted. Thousands of people were killed. Martinique was fifteen hundred miles from Nicaragua, and most Nicaraguan volcanoes were extinct. But that made no difference. The United States congressmen had suddenly become

terrified of volcanoes. Bunau-Varilla, the super-
salesman, had sold Congress on Panama. In 1902,
Congress authorized the president to buy the
French rights to the Panama Canal. At the time, the
president was Theodore Roosevelt.

Theodore Roosevelt was the most exciting president the American people had ever seen. Born to a
wealthy New York family, he had been a brilliant
student at Harvard. He also had been an amateur
boxer, a cowboy, a big-game hunter, and a famous
cavalry leader. He loved poetry and literature and
was also a gifted writer. But mainly Roosevelt was a

PHILIPPE BUNAU-VARILLA AND HIS NICARAGUAN STAMP

PRESIDENT THEODORE ROOSEVELT

man of action. While others talked about projects, he finished them.

Roosevelt was vice president in 1901 when President William McKinley was assassinated. At the age of forty-two, Roosevelt became the youngest president to take office. He was determined to make the United States the greatest power on earth. To achieve that power, he believed America must control the seas. That meant the country must have a strong navy and a canal through Central America. In his very first message to Congress, Roosevelt spoke about an inter-ocean canal: "No single great material work which remains to be undertaken on this continent is of such consequence to the American people."

Every president since Jefferson had talked about building a canal connecting the Atlantic and the Pacific oceans. Now Roosevelt would turn the words into actions.

Events moved quickly under Roosevelt's leadership. His secretary of state, John Hay, started treaty discussions with Colombia. Panama was still a province of Colombia. The United States offered to pay Colombia for the old French canal site. The Colombians held out, hoping to get still more money. In Washington, Roosevelt fumed at the delay. "I do not think [the Colombians] should be allowed to permanently bar one of the future highways of civilization," Roosevelt said to his secretary of state.

In 1903 a revolution broke out in Panama. A group of Panamanians declared their country independent from Colombia. The revolution was a fortunate turn of events for Roosevelt and the United States. Now Secretary of State Hay could deal with a new government eager for American money and American protection.

Secretary of State Hay signed a treaty with the infant republic of Panama. Negotiating for Panama was Frenchman Philippe Bunau-Varilla. The terms of the Hay-Bunau-Varilla Treaty were very favorable to the United States. For Bunau-Varilla, a canal through the Isthmus of Panama would be the completion of a life's work.

With the treaty signed, the incredible task of building the Panama Canal could begin. Armies of workers swarmed to Panama. Steam shovels bigger than dinosaurs were shipped from the United States to Panama. The world watched as the greatest construction project in history began.

But first the Americans had to control the diseases that for hundreds of years had made Panama a graveyard for foreigners. The French had never made an all-out effort to fight disease on the Isthmus. That was one of their major mistakes.

President Roosevelt insisted that the very best medical man in the country take charge of the hospitals in Panama. The Johns Hopkins Medical School recommended Dr. William Gorgas. During the Spanish-American War, Gorgas had served in Havana, Cuba. In the year 1900 there had been fourteen hundred known cases of yellow fever in Havana. Then Gorgas arrived. In 1901, the number of yellow fever cases in Havana dropped to thirty-seven. Gorgas accomplished this miracle by controling mosquitoes. He had studied reports written by

Englishman Ronald Ross and American Walter Reed. Those scientists connected certain tropical diseases with mosquitoes.

Dr. Gorgas studied the mosquitoes of Panama very carefully. Two types of mosquitoes were the major killers. One was a silvery household mosquito that spread yellow fever. The other was a large brown mosquito that lived in swamps. The brown mosquito spread malaria.

Gorgas battled the yellow-fever mosquito first. That mosquito liked to live near people. Gorgas started his efforts in crowded Panama City. Mosquitoes lay their eggs in standing water. Gorgas hoped to eliminate or cover up all standing water in Panama City. He organized teams of Panamanians to prowl the streets looking for barrels, or even tin cans, that might collect rainwater. When found, the containers were turned upside down. Gorgas

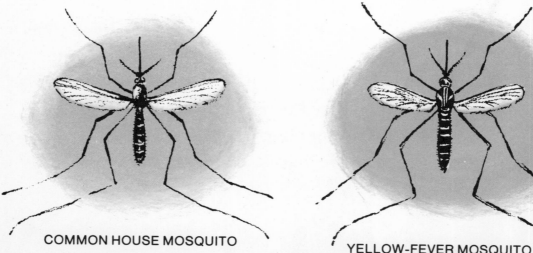

COMMON HOUSE MOSQUITO

YELLOW-FEVER MOSQUITO
(Aëdes aegypti)

ordered all drinking-water tanks in the city to be kept covered. He knew that even the water dish for a pet was a place where mosquitoes could lay eggs. The doctor insisted that mosquito netting be provided for workers' beds, and that screens cover every window on government buildings.

Soon the number of cases of yellow fever in Panama City dropped sharply. Next, Gorgas attacked the malaria-spreading mosquito. That fight would be more difficult. Those mosquitoes lived in the millions of acres of swamps that covered the work sites. To drain those swamps, Gorgas would need the cooperation of the engineers and builders. But many of those men thought that Gorgas was a crackpot. The engineers complained that the doctor was more interested in mosquitoes than he was in sick people. Connecting mosquitoes with disease was a new idea.

DR. WILLIAM GORGAS

Roosevelt had appointed a chief engineer named John Wallace to take charge of the canal project. The president ordered Wallace to "make the dirt fly."

Wallace tried to make the dirt fly. But never in his life had he encountered anything as difficult as digging into the soil of Panama. Engineers call a channel dug through a mountain a "cut." Plans for the Panama Canal included digging a huge cut through a mountain called Culebra. That mountain had been a nightmare for French workers. An American named Plume described to a Senate committee the troubles the French had at Culebra. "The whole top of the hill is covered with boiling springs. It is composed of clay that is utterly impossible for a man to throw off his shovel once he gets it on. He had to have a little scraper to get it off."

Americans attacked Mount Culebra with huge steam shovels. But the scoop parts of the shovels became jammed with sticky mud. Workers often had to shovel out the steam shovels. And even though the mud was sticky, it would still slide back into a freshly dug trench. Digging the Culebra Cut was as frustrating for the Americans as it had been for the French.

MUD SLIDE
IN CULEBRA
CUT.

If the Panama ooze was not enough, the project soon became bogged down in paperwork. The government in faraway Washington demanded reports on everything done in Panama. Forms were required to perform the smallest task. Before a foreman could get a keg of nails he had to fill out a form in triplicate. Carpenters were forbidden to saw boards more than ten feet long without a signed permit. The project was drowning in Panama mud and government red tape.

The exasperated chief engineer John Wallace quit his job. Wallace had always hated Panama. He lived in constant terror of the many diseases. It was said that Wallace had brought his own coffin to Panama with him just in case his body had to be shipped back home.

Wallace was replaced by John Stevens. Stevens was a railroad engineer who was as hard as steel. As a young man, the powerfully built Stevens had worked as a laborer.

John Stevens took over a project that was about to fail. The morale of the workers was dismal. The engineers and foremen had no plans and no direction. The work force of seventeen thousand men were standing around waiting for someone to tell them what to do.

Stevens plunged into his work. He was not the kind of engineer who would sit behind a desk all day. He put on boots and overalls and trudged up and down the canal line barking out orders. "There are three diseases on the Isthmus," he told the workers. "Yellow fever, malaria, and cold feet. And the worst of these is cold feet."

First Stevens acted on the government red tape that had tied up so much work. After visiting the

Culebra Cut, he found "nobody working but the ants and the typists." Stevens eliminated the red tape by sending the government clerks and typists home. Bookkeepers in Washington complained, but President Roosevelt backed Stevens. He was a man who could "make the dirt fly."

But Stevens was in no hurry to dig. He thought an eagerness to dig was one of Wallace's biggest mistakes. Instead, Stevens concentrated on *preparing* to dig. He knew that the mightiest steam shovels in the world were useless if the dirt they dug was not hauled away immediately. So he concentrated on building railroad tracks and roads to and from the huge digging machines. Stevens once wrote, "To get maximum efficiency out of any loading machine, steam shovel, or dragline the boom must be kept swinging every possible minute of the time. And this can be accomplished by keeping empty cars or trucks always at hand to receive their loads from the machine."

To improve morale, Stevens improved life for the Isthmus workers. He built churches, hospitals, schools, and mess halls. In all, some five thousand new buildings went up under his leadership. He also organized band concerts and even formed a Panama

JOHN F.
WALLACE

JOHN
STEVENS

baseball league. Each campsite on the canal line had a home team. The two best teams played in an all-Panama World Series.

The greatest morale problem on the Isthmus was the fear of disease. Stevens cooperated with Dr. Gorgas, and joined his war against malaria-spreading mosquitoes. This meant spending time and money draining the swamps near the canal line. But where the health of his workers was concerned, Stevens was never afraid to spend money. During his first year, Dr. Gorgas' entire budget was only fifty thousand dollars. Under Stevens, Gorgas was allowed to spend ninety thousand for screens alone.

Soon Dr. Gorgas won his war against disease on the Isthmus of Panama. What once had been a graveyard for foreign workers became, as Roosevelt said, "as safe as a health resort." Amazingly, the death rate from disease among workers in Panama dropped lower than the death rate for workers in any other American city. Dr. Gorgas had accomplished a miracle.

Perhaps John Stevens' greatest contribution to the Panama Canal was a major change in construction plans. When Stevens first arrived, engineers were digging a sea-level canal. This meant they were digging one long, deep trench between the two oceans. Newspapers in the United States called the canal the "Big Ditch."

After a few months on the job, Stevens became convinced that a sea-level canal was madness. Workers would have to dig the Big Ditch through a mountain range in the middle of the Isthmus. Such a monstrous cut could take ten years to dig. Also, a roaring river called the Chagres ran through the mountain range. One writer called the Chagres "the lion in the path" of the Panama Canal.

Stevens backed a plan that would tame the Chagres River and eliminate the need for cutting through the mountain range. He proposed building a lock canal. Locks are water-filled chambers with giant doors on either end. When a ship passes through a lock, canal engineers open the front door of the first lock to allow the ship to sail into the chamber. The door is closed behind the ship and engineers pump more water into the chamber. The added water raises the ship up to the height of the next lock. Step by step and lock by lock, a ship can be lifted over a mountain range and lowered back down again. But on top of the mountain range in Panama, the Chagres River roared. Stevens planned to dam the Chagres, thereby creating a huge man-made lake. Ships passing through the canal could then be raised to the top of the mountain range by a series of locks, sail across the man-made lake, and then be lowered by another series of locks.

Stevens traveled to Washington and advised Congress to build a lock canal. After much debate, Congress agreed. The plans for building the Big Ditch were scrapped.

With work going smoothly, President Roosevelt visited the canal site. He was delighted to see progress being made on his favorite project. A photographer snapped a famous picture of Roosevelt

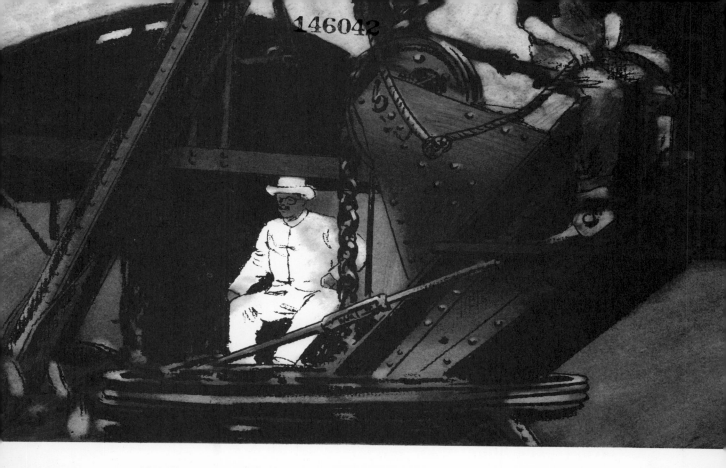

sitting at the controls of a ninety-five-ton steam shovel.

Then, in 1907, John Stevens suddenly quit his job as chief engineer for the canal project. His reasons for quitting were not clear. But it was known that he could make far more money supervising engineering projects in the United States.

In Washington, Theodore Roosevelt was furious over losing his chief engineer. Roosevelt roared, "I propose now to put it in charge of men who will stay on the job till I get tired of having them there. . . . I shall turn it over to the army."

Colonel George Goethals became the third and last chief engineer of the Panama Canal construction project. At first, the workmen were afraid of having an army man as their boss. Stevens had been very popular with the workers. But although Goethals had spent a lifetime in the army, he had always been a member of the Corps of Engineers. He disliked stuffy uniforms and had not marched in a parade since he was a young officer. Soon Goethals became as popular among the workers as Stevens had been.

Roosevelt chose Goethals because he had had experience building canals with locks. But no engineer in history had ever tackled a job like building the enormous locks of the Panama Canal. The plans called for constructing three sets of locks. The locks were to be built in pairs. That would allow ships to pass through the canal in both directions at the same time. Each lock was to be 1,000 feet long, 110 feet wide, and 70 feet deep.

Building these monster locks took four years. Enough concrete was poured into each lock to build the largest of the Egyptian pyramids. When one lock was nearly complete, artist Joseph Pennell climbed to the floor of the empty chamber to draw it.

He was so awed by the huge size of the chamber he was in, that for a time he was unable to draw.

Each one of the giant chambers had swinging doors at either end. The doors were built of steel and weighed thousands of tons. Yet to seal water they had to fit together as precisely as the gears on a Swiss watch. When finished, the locks worked even better than the engineers had dreamed. They are still functioning perfectly today.

LOCKS BETWEEN GATUN LAKE (UPPER RIGHT) & ATLANTIC (LOWER LEFT)

PACIFIC SIDE

CANAL & GATUN LAKE ABOUT 85 FT. ABOVE SEA LEVEL

ATLANTIC SIDE

PEDRO MIGUEL LOCKS

MIRAFLORES LOCKS

GATUN LOCKS

Even though the building plan was changed to include locks, the frustrating Culebra Cut still had to be dug. Goethals tackled the problem of constant mud slides by keeping an army of workers digging away at the cut. Sixty locomotives, each pulling thirty cars, hauled dirt away from the mountain around the clock. The dirt taken from Mount Culebra was used to dam up the Chagres River and create the man-made lake. When finally completed, the Culebra Cut looked like part of the Grand Canyon. It was eight miles long, five hundred feet wide, and more than one hundred feet deep. Today it is called the Gaillard Cut, and mud still slides off its walls. The Gaillard Cut has to be dredged constantly.

In 1913 more than 43,000 people worked on the Panama Canal. They came from every corner of the world. Records show that men from ninety-seven different countries worked on the project. About three-quarters of the workers were black people from the West Indies.

For ten years, workers and machines gouged out the earth across the Isthmus of Panama. Finally the money, brains, muscle, and sweat that were poured into the canal project were rewarded.

THE STEAMER ANCON STARTS INTO CULEBRA CUT, (NOW THE GAILLARD CUT) AUG. 15, 1914.

At nine-fifteen on the morning of August 15, 1914, the huge doors of the Gatun Lock swung open. A tiny cargo ship called the *Ancon* inched into the enormous chamber. Thousands of spectators had gathered to watch. They cheered as the ship churned past them. The *Ancon* was the first commercial ship to pass through the Panama Canal. Thousands more would follow.

Today the Panama Canal is busier than ever. Each year twelve thousand ships clear its locks. The canal is about forty-seven miles long. A trip through it takes a ship fifteen hours. Because the canal is so busy, about half of those hours are spent as waiting time. To go through the canal, a ship's captain pays a fee based on the tonnage of his ship. Any kind of ship is allowed to enter. In 1928 an adventurer named Halliburton swam through the canal. He was charged a fee of thirty-six cents.

The designers of the Panama Canal had great vision. They built the lock chambers large enough to accommodate the huge ships they believed would cross the oceans in the future. Even World War II battleships could fit through the canal. Only in recent times have ships been designed that are too large for the Panama Canal.

But the Panama Canal is getting old. Engineers discuss digging a new Central American canal some day. A favorite site among engineers is Nicaragua.

Since its opening, the Panama Canal has been operated by Americans. The 1903 Hay-Bunau-Varilla Treaty gave the United States a strip of land ten miles wide across the Isthmus. That strip of land is called the Canal Zone. According to the old treaty, the United States had the right to stay in the Canal Zone forever. But Panamanians had always resented a treaty negotiated by a French engineer and signed when their country was only fifteen days old. In 1977 the United States and Panama signed a new treaty. That treaty turned over many functions of the canal to Panama. The new treaty will give Panama complete control over the canal in the year 2000.

The Panama Canal's opening in 1914 was a four-hundred-year-old dream come true. The American canal followed the same course as the French canal line. The French canal took the route of the old Panama Railroad, which followed the even older Spanish mule path. With the completion of the canal, the Isthmus of Panama was once more the crossroads of the world.

Visitors going through the Panama Canal today are still impressed by the magnitude of the 1904-to-1914 construction project. The walls of the Gaillard Cut are two and three times taller than the ships passing through. It is difficult to believe the incredible canyon is man-made. It is also difficult to believe that the giant doors of the locks still yawn open and seal shut flawlessly after seventy years of constant operation. The Panama Canal stands as a monument to the courage of its builders. They entered a forbidding jungle and created an engineering miracle.

About the Author

R. Conrad Stein was born and grew up in Chicago. He enlisted in the Marine Corps at the age of eighteen and served for three years. He then attended the University of Illinois where he received a bachelor's degree in history. He later studied in Mexico, earning an advanced degree from the University of Guanajuato. Mr. Stein is the author of many other books, articles, and short stories written for young people.

Mr. Stein now lives in Pennsylvania with his wife, Deborah Kent, who is also a writer of books for young readers.

About the Artist

Keith Neely attended the School of the Art Institute of Chicago and received a Bachelor of Fine Arts degree with honors from the Art Center College of Design, where he majored in illustration. He has worked as an art director, designer, and illustrator and has taught advertising illustration and advertising design at Biola College in La Mirada, California. Mr. Neely is currently a freelance illustrator whose work has appeared in numerous magazines, books, and advertisements. He lives with his wife and five children in Flossmoor, Illinois, a suburb of Chicago.